Brothers &
Builders

By Joseph Fort Newton

Copyright © 2021 Lamp of Trismegistus. All rights reserved. No part of this publication may be reproduced or transmitted in any form or by any means, electronic or mechanical, including photocopying, recording, or by any information storage and retrieval system, without permission in writing from Lamp of Trismegistus. Reviewers may quote brief passages.

ISBN: 978-1-63118-506-9

Foundations of Freemasonry Series

Other Books in this Series and Related Titles

Masonic and Rosicrucian History by M P Hall & H Voorhis (978-1-63118-486-4)

The Kabbalah of Masonry & Related Writings by E Levi &c (978-1-63118-453-6)

Some Deeper Aspects of Masonic Symbolism by A E Waite (978-1-63118-461-1)

Masonic Symbolism of King Solomon's Temple by A Mackey &c (978-1-63118-442-0)

The Old Past Master by Carl H Claudy (978-1-63118-464-2)

The Influence of Pythagoras on Freemasonry and Other Essays (978-1-63118-404-8)

The Symbols and Legends of Masonry by C H Vail (978-1-63118-504-5)

Rosicrucians and Speculative Masonry in the Seventeenth Century (978-1-63118-489-5)

The Two Great Pillars of Boaz and Jachin by A Mackey &c (978-1-63118-433-8)

The Regius Poem or Halliwell Manuscript by King Solomon (978-1-63118-447-5)

The Lost Keys of Freemasonry or The Secret of Hiram Abiff (978-1-63118-427-7)

The Master Mason's Handbook by J S M Ward (978-1-63118-474-1)

Masonic Symbolism of the Apron & the Altar by various (978-1-63118-428-4)

Symbolism and Discourses on the Entered Apprentice, Fellowcraft and Master Mason Blue Lodge Degrees by various (978-1-63118-413-0)

Freemasonry & Catholicism by Max Heindel (978-1-63118-508-3)

American Indian Freemasonry by A C Parker (978-1-63118-460-4)

Freemasonry, Mithraism and the Ancient Mysteries by various (978-1-63118-407-9)

The Ceremony of Initiation: Analysis & Commentary (978-1-63118-473-4)

Masonic Life of George Washington by Albert G Mackey (978-1-63118-457-4)

The Janeites, The Man Who Would Be King and Other Stories of Freemasonry by Rudyard Kipling (978-1-63118-480-2)

Audio Versions are also available on Audible, Amazon and Apple

Other Books in this Series and Related Titles

Rosicrucian Rules, Secret Signs, Codes and Symbols by various (978-1-63118-488-8)

History and Teachings of the Rosicrucians by W W Westcott &c (978-1-63118-487-1)

The Mysteries of Freemasonry & the Druids by various (978-1-63118-444-4)

Masonic Symbolism in Shakespeare by Clegg & McDaniel (978-1-63118-472-7)

Ancient Egyptian Mysteries and Hieroglyphics, Modern Freemasonry & Initiation of the Pyramid by Evans, Newton, M P Hall &c (978-1-63118-430-7)

Freemasonry and the Egyptian Mysteries by C. W. Leadbeater (978-1-63118-456-7)

Qabbalistic Teachings and the Tree of Life by M P Hall (978-1-63118-482-6)

Symbolism of the Corner Stone, the North East Corner and the Religious & Masonic Symbolism of Stones by Albert G Mackey &c (978-1-63118-412-3)

Cloud Upon the Sanctuary by K. Eckartshausen (978-1-63118-438-3)

An Outline of Theosophy by C. W. Leadbeater (978-1-63118-452-9)

Royal Arch, Capitular and Cryptic Masonry by Waite &c (978-1-63118-425-3)

The Psalms of Solomon by King Solomon (978-1-63118-439-0)

The Book of Wisdom of Solomon by King Solomon (978-1-63118-502-1)

Masonic Symbolism of Easter and the Christ in Masonry (978-1-63118-434-5)

The Odes of Solomon by King Solomon (978-1-63118-503-8)

Ancient Mysteries and Secret Societies by M P Hall (978-1-63118-410-9)

The Golden Verses of Pythagoras: Five Translations (978-1-63118-479-6)

A Few Masonic Sermons by A. C. Ward &c (978-1-63118-435-2)

The Story and Legend of Hiram Abiff by Albert G Mackey &c (978-1-63118-411-6)

The Legend of the Holy Grail and its Connection with Templars and Freemasons by A E Waite (978-1-63118-462-8)

Audio versions are also available on Audible, Amazon and Apple

Table of Contents

Series Introduction...7

Brothers & Builders:
Eight Addresses on the Basis and Spirit of Freemasonry

Introduction...9

Chapter I: *The Altar*...16

Chapter II: *The Holy Bible*...22

Chapter III: *The Square*...28

Chapter IV: *The Compasses*...35

Chapter V: *The Level and the Plumb*...41

Chapter VI: *The Master's Piece*...47

Chapter VII: *The Rite of Destitution*...54

Chapter VIII: *The Inn of Year's End*...61

INTRODUCTION

From the beginning of Modern Freemasonry's birthdate of 1717, the intelligentsia of humanity have found refuge for safe reflection within the walls of the fraternity. Masonic writers have produced a nearly incalculable amount of written musings on a multitude of esoteric and philosophical subjects, as they relate to the ancient mysteries that Freemasonry currently storehouses. Sadly, most of it appears to have sat largely unread, as American Freemasonry in particular, continues to transform itself into something that bears little resemblance to what it was originally designed to be. The true essence of Freemasonry is not that of blind patriotism or a single-minded national religion but one of Universal Brotherhood and altruism, designed for the betterment not just of its members but of society as a whole. In particular, for those who are not members of the fraternity, as Freemasonry has always acted as a beacon, to help guide humanity through darker times, with the hopes that one day we will collectively reach a truly enlightened age.

It's not uncommon for new members joining the fraternity to find little education within the walls of many modern lodges, in spite of so much written material available to the membership. Many older members are not simply uneducated with regards to real Masonic history and symbology, not to mention the vast arena of related subjects, but they are disinterested in all of it, as well.

Lamp of Trismegistus is doing its part to help preserve humanity's Masonic history by making some of these classics available to those students who are seeking to unearth the knowledge of these ancient colossi. As such, Lamp of Trismegistus offers its readers highlights of Masonic study, culled from a variety of authors and viewpoints, with the hope bringing education back into the fraternity. So, be sure to check out other titles in our *Foundations of Freemasonry Series* as well as our *Theosophical Classics, Occult Fiction, Paranormal Research Series, Esoteric Classics, Supernatural Fiction, Studies in Buddhism* and our *Christian Apocrypha Series* as well as numerous other subjects; and, don't be afraid to let a little altruism into your own heart or even into your Lodge. You can also download the audio versions of many of these titles from Audible, Amazon or Apple, for learning on the go.

BROTHERS AND BUILDERS

INTRODUCTION

I.

The basis of Freemasonry is a Faith which can neither be demonstrated nor argued down - Faith in God the wise Master-Builder by whose grace we live, and whose will we must learn and obey. Upon this basis Masonry builds, digging deep into the realities of life, using great and simple symbols to enshrine a Truth too vast for words, seeking to exalt men, to purify and refine their lives, to ennoble their hopes; in short to build men and then make them Brothers and Builders.

There is no need - nay, it were idle - to argue in behalf of this profound and simple Faith, because any view of life which is of value is never maintained, much less secured, by debate. For though God, which is the name we give to the mystery and meaning of life, may be revealed in experience He cannot be uttered, and in a conflict of words we easily lose the sense of the unutterable God, the Maker of Heaven and earth and all that in them is, before whom silence is wisdom and wonder becomes worship. It is enough to appeal to the natural and uncorrupted sense of humanity, its right reason, its moral intuition, its spiritual instinct. Long before logic was born man, looking out over the rivers, the hills and the far horizon, and into the still depths of the night sky, knew that there was Something here before he was here; Something which will be here when he is gone.

Happily we are not confronted by a universe which mocks our intelligence and aspiration, and a system of things which is interpretable as far as we can go by our minds, must itself be the expression and embodiment of Mind. What is equally wonderful and awful, lending divinity to our dust, is that the Mind within and behind all the multicolored wonder of the world is akin to our own, since the world is both intelligible by and responsive to our thought - a mystery not an enigma. And, if one door yields to our inquiry, and another door opens at our knock, and another and another, it only requires a certain daring of spirit - that is, Faith - to believe that, if not yet by us, why, then, by those who come after us, or, mayhap, by ourselves in some state of being in which we shall no longer be restrained by the weaknesses of mortality, or befogged by the illusions of time, the mind of man shall find itself at home and unafraid in the universe of God, a son and citizen of a City that hath foundations.

II.

What, now, precisely, does this profound faith mean to us here? Obviously, it means that we are here in the world to do something, to build something, to be something - not simply to pass the time or to wear out shoes - and what we do and build ought to express and perpetuate our personality, our character. There is one kind of immortality which we should earn in the world, by adding something of worth to the world, by so building ourselves into the order of things that whatever immortality this world may have, our life and labour shall share in it. Once, in the south of England, I heard a little poem which seemed to me to have in it a bit of final philosophy-not a great poem but telling a great truth:

> *"The good Lord made the earth and sky,*
> *The rivers and the sea, and me,*
> *He made no roads; but here am I as happy as can be.*
> *It's just as though He'd said to me,*
> *'John, there's the job for thee.'"*

The idea in the rhyme is that in a very real sense God has completed nothing; not because He has not the power or the will to do so, but out of a kind of respect for men, so to put it, offering us a share in His creative work. He makes no roads, He builds no houses. True, he provides us with the material; He supplies us with firm foundations - and models of every shape of beauty - but the road and the house must be the work of man. Our good and wise poet, Edwin Markham, was right when he wrote:

> *"We men of earth have here the stuff*
> *Of Paradise - we have enough!*
> *We need no other thing to build*
> *The stairs into the Unfulfilled -*
> *No other ivory for the doors -*
> *No other marble for the floors -*
> *No other cedar for the beam*
> *And dome of man's immortal dream.*
> *Here on the paths of everyday -*
> *Here on the common human way -*
> *Is all the busy gods would take*
> *To build a heaven, to mould and make*
> *New Edens. Ours the stuff sublime*
> *To build Eternity in time."*

Not only are we here in the world to build something, but we are here to build upon the Will of God, in obedience to His purpose and design. The truth of a will within and behind everything is a truth which has far too little place in our lives; hence our impatience, our restlessness, and our sense of futility. Yet this truth of the Will of God as final has been the strength and solace of man in all his great days. The first fact of experience, if not the last truth of philosophy, is that the world has a mind of its own, which we call the will and purpose of God. Manifestly the only man who builds rightly is the man who builds with due regard for the laws, forces and conditions of the world in which he lives.

Not one of us would trust ourselves to a house which had been built casually and haphazard. We demand of a wall that it shall have been built with respect to the centre of gravity of this earth, and to the position of the polar star. Our work, if it is to be of any worth, must be in harmony with the nature of things; and this is equally true when we think of the House of the Spirit not built with hands, but which, none the less, we are set to build in the midst of the years. Here also we build wisely only when we build in harmony with the Will of God as we believe and see it. All history enforces the truth that there is a Will, holy and inexorable, which in the end passes judgment upon our human undertakings. Men do not make laws; they discover them. Faith in God advises us, warns us, to regard the revelations of the moral, as well as the physical, Will of God, else our proudest fabric will totter to ruin.

Therefore we are here in the world to build upon the Will of God with the help of God, invoking His help in words of prayer and worship, but also in our efforts and acts of obedience, and proving ourselves worthy of that help, and retaining it, by keeping in the midst of it by humble fidelity. A wise man, especially a Freemason - if he knows his art - will rebuke himself and recall himself from any vagrant lapse or prolonged neglect, lest he go too far. Here is a matter which even the best of us too often forget. God no more wishes us to live without His aid than He wishes us to live without air. He is the breath of our spirit. Truly has it been said that the final truth about man is not that way down in the depths he is alone; but that in the depths he is face to face with God.

Long ago it was said: "Except the Lord build the house they labour in vain that build it." What the Psalmist means is that the great things in the world are not accomplished by man, either by his anxieties or by his ingenuities. By these lower, lesser faculties by cunning, by cleverness - we may achieve small and passing things. The truth is, rather, that the great things, the enduring things, are accomplished - not, indeed, apart from us, and yet not wholly as the result of our efforts - by One wiser than ourselves by whom we are employed in the fulfilment of a design larger than we have planned and nobler than we have dreamed. Those of our race who have wrought the most beautiful and enduring works confess themselves to have been used by a Hand and a Will other than their own, as if caught up into the rhythm of "one vast life that moves and cannot die."

Here is no abstract and unreal platitude, but a truth, a fact, a source to which we may apply a daily test, and which we need to invoke if we are to face the difficulties and embarrassments - aye, the tragedies - of these our days and years. Even the strongest of us need such resource the better to confront the issues of the day, as well as to face the vaster problems and mysteries which lie on all the horizons of our life.

III.

Such is the foundation of Freemasonry, and the faith by which it makes us builders upon the Will of God and by His help, and brothers one of another. Upon this foundation is erected an elaborate allegory of human life in all its varied aspects: the Lodge a symbol of the world in which man lives, moves and goes forth to his labour; initiation our birth into a world in which we are to learn morality and charity; if counted worthy passing out of youth into manhood with its wider knowledge and heavier responsibilities; and finally, if we have integrity and courage, the discovery that we are citizens of Eternity in time: an ideal world ruled by love, wisdom, strength and beauty. It is a great day for a young man when Masonry reveals its meaning to him, unveiling its plan of life, its purpose, and its prophecy of a Temple of Brotherhood.

A great Freemason of Scotland, who recently climbed ahead to work up in the dome of the Temple, left us a legacy of inspiration and instruction in a book which is at once a mentor and a memorial: "Speculative Masonry," by A. S. MacBride, Lodge Progress, Glasgow. Even now it is a classic of our literature, a light to lead his Brethren toward the truth after he has vanished from among us. The book is wise rather than clever, beautiful rather than brilliant; but there is hardly a page that does not yield some insight to illumine, some epigram to haunt the mind. The beauty of the book is inwrought, not decorative; in the build of its thought even more than in the turn of its sentences, and still more in its spirit in which spiritual vision and practical wisdom are blended. There are passages of singular nobility, as witness this one on the Great Landmark:

"Why is Masonry here, in this world of selfishness and strife? Wherefore has it been developed, amid war and incessant conflict, along the lines of peace and love; and so marvelously moulded and developed that in every land it is now known and by every race made welcome? Has all this been done that it may live for itself alone? No, there, on its Trestleboard is the Plan of the Great Architect and its mission is to work out that plan. Out of the rough hard quarries of a quarrelling humanity it has to build a Temple of Brotherhood and Peace. This Temple is the Great Landmark - the highest and grandest ideal of Masonry. To build, strengthen and beautify it, we must bring in the aid of all the arts and sciences, apply every resource that civilization and progress can give us, and exercise all the powers and gifts with which we have been endowed.

"What nobler work can we be engaged in, Brethren ? Yet, how far we are, as a rule, from understanding it. We seem to be groping in the dark. Yet, it is ignorance more than unwillingness that hinders the work. Like the ingenious craftsman at the building of the Temple at Jerusalem, we appear to be without plan and instruction, while, in reality, our plan and instruction lie in the work itself. Then, like him, we shall some day have our reward, and will gratefully exclaim: Thank God, I have marked well."

CHAPTER I
The Altar

A Masonic Lodge is a symbol of the world as it was thought to be in the olden time. Our ancient Brethren had a profound insight when they saw that the world is a Temple, over-hung by a starry canopy by night, lighted by the journeying sun by day, wherein man goes forth to his labor on a checker-board of lights and shadows, joys and sorrows, seeking to reproduce on earth the law and order of heaven. The visible world was but a picture or reflection of the invisible, and at its centre stood the Altar of sacrifice, obligation, and adoration.

While we hold a view of the world very unlike that held by our ancient Brethren - knowing it to be round, not flat and square - yet their insight is still true. The whole idea was that man, if he is to build either a House of Faith or an order of Society that is to endure, must imitate the laws and principles of the world in which he lives. That is also our dream and design; the love of it ennobles our lives; it is our labor and our worship. To fulfill it, we too need wisdom and help from above; and so at the centre of our Lodge stands the same Altar - older than all temples, as old as life itself - a focus of faith and fellowship, at once a symbol and shrine of that unseen element of thought and yearning that all men are aware of and which no one can define.

Upon this earth there is nothing more impressive than the silence of a company of human beings bowed together at an altar. No thoughtful man but at some time has mused over the meaning of this great adoring habit of humanity, and the wonder of it deepens the longer he ponders it. The instinct which thus draws men together in prayer is the strange power which has drawn together the stones of great cathedrals, where the mystery of God is embodied. So far as we know, man is the only being on our planet that pauses to pray, and the wonder of his worship tells us more about him than any other fact. By some deep necessity of his nature he is a seeker after God, and in moments of sadness or longing, in hours of tragedy or terror, he lays aside his tools and looks out over the far horizon.

The history of the Altar in the life of man is a story more fascinating than any fiction. Whatever else man may have been - cruel, tyrannous, or vindictive - the record of his long search for God is enough to prove that he is not wholly base, not altogether an animal. Rites horrible, and often bloody, may have been a part of his early ritual, but if the history of past ages had left us nothing but the memory of a race at prayer, it would have left us rich. And so, following the good custom of the men which were of old, we set up an Altar in the Lodge, lifting up hands in prayer, moved thereto by the ancient need and aspiration of our humanity. Like the men who walked in the grey years agone, our need is for the living God to hallow these our days and years, even to the last ineffable homeward sigh which men call death.

The earliest Altar was a rough, unhewn stone set up, like the stone which Jacob set up at Bethel when his dream of a ladder, on which angels were ascending and descending, turned his lonely bed into a house of God and a gate of heaven. Later, as faith became more refined, and the idea of sacrifice grew in meaning, the Altar was built of hewn stone - cubical in form - cut, carved, and often beautifully wrought, on which men lavished jewels and priceless gifts, deeming nothing too costly to adorn the place of prayer. Later still, when men erected a Temple dedicated and adorned as the House of God among men, there were two altars, one of sacrifice, and one of incense. The altar of sacrifice, where slain beasts were offered, stood in front of the Temple; the altar of incense, on which burned the fragrance of worship, stood within. Behind all was the far withdrawn Holy place into which only the high priest might enter.

As far back as we can go the Altar was the centre of human Society, and an object of peculiar sanctity by virtue of that law of association by which places and things are consecrated. It was a place of refuge for the hunted or the tormented - criminals or slaves - and to drag them away from it by violence was held to be an act of sacrilege, since they were under the protection of God. At the Altar marriage rites were solemnized, and treaties made or vows taken in its presence were more holy and binding than if made elsewhere, because there man invoked God as witness. In all the religions of antiquity, and especially among the peoples who worshipped the Light, it was the usage of both priests and people to pass round the Altar, following the course of the sun - from the East, by way of the South, to the West - singing hymns of praise as a part of their worship. Their ritual was thus an allegorical picture of the truth which underlies all religion - that man must live on earth in harmony with the rhythm and movement of heaven.

From facts and hints such as these we begin to see the meaning of the Altar in Masonry, and the reason for its position in the Lodge. In English Lodges, as in the French and Scottish Rites, it stands in front of the Master in the East. In the York Rite, so called, it is placed in the centre of the Lodge - more properly a little to the East of the centre - about which all Masonic activities revolve. It is not simply a necessary piece of furniture, a kind of table intended to support the Holy Bible, the Square and Compasses. Alike by its existence and its situation it identifies Masonry as a religious institution, and yet its uses are not exactly the same as the offices of an Altar in a cathedral or a shrine. Here is a fact often overlooked, and we ought to get it clearly in our minds.

The position of the Altar in the Lodge is not accidental, but profoundly significant. For, while Masonry is not a religion, it is religious in its faith and basic principles, no less than in its spirit and purpose. And yet it is not a Church. Nor does it attempt to do what the Church is trying to do. If it were a Church its Altar would be in the East and its ritual would be altered accordingly. That is to say, Masonry is not a Religion, much less a sect, but a Worship in which all men can unite, because it does not undertake to explain, or dogmatically to settle in detail, those issues by which men are divided. Beyond the Primary, fundamental facts of faith it does not go. With the philosophy of those facts, and the differences and disputes growing out of them, it has not to do. In short, the position of the Altar in the Lodge is a symbol of what Masonry believes the Altar should be in actual life, a centre of union and fellowship, and not a cause of division, as is now so often the case. It does not seek uniformity of opinion, but it does seek fraternity of spirit, leaving each one free to fashion his own philosophy of ultimate truth. As we may read in the Constitutions of 1723:

"A Mason is obliged, by his Tenure, to obey the moral Law; and if he rightly understands the Art, he will never be a stupid Atheist, nor an irreligious Libertine. But though in ancient Times Masons were charged in every Country to be of the Religion of that Country or Nation, whatever it was, yet 'tis now thought more expedient only to oblige them to that Religion in which all Men agree, leaving their particular Opinions to themselves; that is, to be good Men and true, or Men of Honour and Honesty, by whatever Denominations or Persuasions they may be distinguished; whereby Masonry becomes the Centre of Union, and the Means of conciliating true Friendship among Persons that must have remained at a perpetual Distance."

Surely those are memorable words, a Magna Charta of friendship and fraternity. Masonry goes hand in hand with religion until religion enters the field of sectarian feud, and there it stops; because Masonry seeks to unite men, not to divide them. Here, then, is the meaning of the Masonic Altar and its position in the Lodge. It is, first of all, an Altar of Faith - the deep, eternal faith which underlies all creeds and overarches all sects; faith in God, in the moral law, and in the life everlasting. Faith in God is the cornerstone and the key-stone of Freemasonry. It is the first truth and the last, the truth that makes all other truths true, without which life is a riddle and fraternity a futility. For, apart from God the Father, our dream of the Brotherhood of Man is as vain as all the vain things proclaimed of Solomon-a fiction having no basis or hope in fact.

At the same time, the Altar of Masonry is an Altar of Freedom - not freedom from faith, but freedom of faith. Beyond the fact of the reality of God it does not go, allowing every man to think of God according to his experience of life and his vision of truth. It does not define God, much less dogmatically determine how and what men shall think or believe about God. There dispute and division begin. As a matter of fact, Masonry is not speculative at all, but operative, or rather co-operative. While all its teaching implies the Fatherhood of God, yet its ritual does not actually affirm that truth, still less make it a test of fellowship. Behind this silence lies a deep and wise reason. Only by the practice of Brotherhood do men realize the Divine Fatherhood, as a true-hearted poet has written

"No man could tell me what my soul might be;
I sought for God, and He eluded me;
I sought my Brother out, and found all three."

Hear one fact more, and the meaning of the Masonic Altar will be plain. Often one enters a great Church, like Westminster Abbey, and finds it empty, or only a few people in the pews here and there, praying or in deep thought. They are sitting quietly, each without reference to others, seeking an opportunity for the soul to be alone, to communicate with mysteries greater than itself, and find healing for the bruisings of life. But no one ever goes to a Masonic Altar alone. No one bows before it at all except when the Lodge is open and in the presence of his Brethren. It is an Altar of Fellowship, as if to teach us that no man can learn the truth for another, and no man can learn it alone. Masonry brings men together in mutual respect, sympathy, and good-will, that we may learn in love the truth that is hidden by apathy and lost by hate.

For the rest, let us never forget - what has been so often and so sadly forgotten - that the most sacred Altar on earth is the soul of man - your soul and mine; and that the Temple and its ritual are not ends in themselves, but beautiful means to the end that every human heart may be a sanctuary of faith, a shrine of love, an altar of purity, pity, and unconquerable hope.

CHAPTER II
The Holy Bible

Upon the Altar of every Masonic Lodge, supporting the Square and Compasses, lies the Holy Bible. The old, familiar Book, so beloved by so many generations, is our Volume of Sacred Law and a Great Light in Masonry. The Bible opens when the Lodge opens; it closes when the Lodge closes. No Lodge can transact its own business, much less initiate candidates into its mysteries, unless the Book of Holy Law lies open upon its Altar. Thus the book of the Will of God rules the Lodge in its labours, as the Sun rules the day, making its work a worship.

The history of the Bible in the life and symbolism of Masonry is a story too long to recite here. Nor can any one tell it as we should like to know it. Just when, where, and by whom the teaching and imagery of the Bible were wrought into Freemasonry, no one can tell. Anyone can have his theory, but no one can be dogmatic. As the Craft laboured in the service of the Church during the cathedral-building period, it is not difficult to account for the Biblical coloring of its thought, even in days when the Bible was not widely distributed, and before the discovery of printing. Anyway, we can take such facts as we are able to find, leaving further research to learn further truth.

The Bible is mentioned in some of the old Manuscripts of the Craft long before the revival of Masonry in 1717, as the book upon which the covenant, or oath, of a Mason was taken; but it is not referred to as a Great Light. For example, in the Harleian Manuscript, dated about 1600, the obligation of an initiate closes with the words: "So help me God, and the holy contents of this Book." In the old Ritual, of which a copy from the Royal Library in

Berlin is given by Krause, there is no mention of the Bible as one of the Lights. It was in England, due largely to the influence of Preston and his fellow workmen, that the Bible came to its place of honour in the Lodge. At any rate, in the rituals of about 1760 it is described as one of the three Great Lights.

No Mason needs to be told what a great place the Bible has in the Masonry of our day. It is central, sovereign, supreme, a master light of all our seeing. From the Altar it pours forth upon the East, the West, and the South its white light of spiritual vision, moral law, and immortal hope. Almost every name found in our ceremonies is a Biblical name, and students have traced about seventy-five references to the Bible in the Ritual of the Craft. But more important than direct references is the fact that the spirit of the Bible, its faith, its attitude toward life, pervades Masonry, like a rhythm or a fragrance. As soon as an initiate enters the Lodge, he hears the words of the Bible recited as an accompaniment to his advance toward the light. Upon the Bible every Mason takes solemn vows of loyalty, of chastity and charity, pledging himself to the practice of the Brotherly Life. Then as he moves forward from one degree to another, the imagery of the Bible becomes familiar and eloquent, and its music sings its way into his heart.

Nor is it strange that it should be so. As faith in God is the corner- stone of the Craft, so, naturally, the book which tells us the purest truth about God is its altar- light. The Temple of King Solomon, about which the history, legends, and symbolism of the Craft are woven, was the tallest temple of the ancient world, not in the grandeur of its architecture but in the greatest of the truths for which it stood. In the midst of ignorant idolatries and debasing superstitions the Temple on Mount Moriah stood for the Unity, Righteousness, and Spirituality of God. Upon no other foundation can men build with any sense of security and permanence when the winds blow and the floods descend. But the Bible is not simply a foundation rock; it is also a quarry in which we find the truths that make us men. As in the old ages of geology rays of sunlight were stored up in vast beds of coal, for the uses of man, so in this old book the light of moral truth is stored to light the mind and warm the heart of man.

Alas, there has been more dispute about the Bible than about any other book, making for schism, dividing men into sects. But Masonry knows a certain secret, almost too simple to be found out, whereby it avoids both intolerance and sectarianism. It is essentially religious, but it is not dogmatic. The fact that the Bible lies open upon its Altar means that man must have some Divine revelation - must seek for a light higher than human to guide and govern him. But Masonry lays down no hard and fast dogma on the subject of revelation. It attempts no detailed interpretation of the Bible. The great Book lies open upon its Altar, and is open for all to read, open for each to interpret for himself. The tie by which our Craft is united is strong, but it allows the utmost liberty of faith and thought. It unites men, not upon a creed bristling with debated issues, but upon the broad, simple truth which underlies all creeds and over-arches all sects - faith in God, the wise Master Builder, for whom and with whom man must work.

Herein our gentle Craft is truly wise, and its wisdom was never more needed than to-day, when the churches are divided and torn by angry debate. However religious teachers may differ in their doctrines, in the Lodge they meet with mutual respect and good-will. At the Altar of Masonry they learn not only toleration, but appreciation. In its air of kindly fellowship, man to man, they discover that the things they have in common are greater than the things that divide. It is the glory of Masonry to teach Unity in essentials, Liberty in details, Charity in all things; and by this sign its spirit must at last prevail. It is the beautiful secret of Masonry that all just men, all devout men, all righteous men are everywhere of one religion, and it seeks to remove the hoodwinks of prejudice and intolerance so that they may recognize each other and work together in the doing of good.

Like everything else in Masonry, the Bible, so rich in symbolism, is itself a symbol - that is, a part taken for the whole. It is a symbol of the Book of Truth, the Scroll of Faith, the Record of the Will of God as man has learned it in the midst of the years - the perpetual revelation of Himself which God has made, and is making, to mankind in every age and land. Thus, by the very honour which Masonry pays to the Bible, it teaches us to revere every Book of Faith in which men find help for to-day and hope for the morrow. For that reason, in a Lodge consisting entirely of Jews, the Old Testament alone may be placed upon the Altar, and in a Lodge in the land of Mohammed the Koran may be used. Whether it be the Gospels of the Christian, the Book of Law of the Hebrew, the Koran of the Mussulman, or the Vedas of the Hindu, it everywhere Masonically conveys the same idea -symbolizing the Will of God revealed to man, taking such faith and vision as he has found into a great fellowship of the seekers and finders of the truth.

Thus Masonry invites to its Altar men of all faiths, knowing that, if they use different names for "the Nameless One of an hundred names," they are yet praying to the one God and Father of all; knowing, also, that while they read different volumes, they are in fact reading the same vast Book of the Faith of Man as revealed in the struggle and tragedy of the race in its quest of God. So that, great and noble as the Bible is, Masonry sees it as a symbol of that eternal, ever-unfolding Book of the Will of God which Lowell described in memorable lines:

> *"Slowly the Bible of the race is writ,*
> *And not on paper leaves nor leaves of stone;*
> *Each age, each kindred, adds a verse to it,*
> *Texts of despair or hope, of joy or moan.*
> *While swings the sea, while mists the mountain shroud,*
> *While thunder's surges burst on cliffs of cloud,*
> *Still at the Prophet's feet the nations sit"*

None the less, while we honour every Book of Faith in which have been recorded the way and Will of God, with us the Bible is supreme, at once the mother-book of our literature and the master-book of the Lodge. Its truth is inwrought in the fiber of our being, with whatsoever else of the good and the true which the past has given us. Its spirit stirs our hearts, like a sweet habit of the blood; its light follows all our way, showing us the meaning and worth of life. Its very words have in them memories, echoes and overtones of voices long since hushed, and its scenery is interwoven with the holiest associations of our lives. Our fathers and mothers read it, finding in it their final reasons for living faithfully and nobly, and it is thus a part of the ritual of the Lodge and the ritual of life.

Every Mason ought not only to honour the Bible as a great Light of the Craft; he ought to read it, live with it, love it, lay its truth to heart and learn what it means to be a man. There is something in the old Book which, if it gets into a man, makes him both gentle and strong, faithful and free, obedient and tolerant, adding to his knowledge virtue, patience, temperance, self-control, brotherly love, and pity. The Bible is as high as the sky and as deep as the grave; its two great characters are God and the Soul, and the story of their eternal life together is its everlasting romance. It is the most human of books, telling us the half- forgotten secrets of our own hearts, our sins, our sorrows, our doubts, our hopes. It is the most Divine of books, telling us that God has made us for Himself, and that our hearts will be restless, unhappy and lonely until we learn to rest in Him whose Will is our peace.

> "He hath showed thee, O man, what is good; and what doth the Lord require of thee, but to do justly, to love mercy, and to walk humbly with thy God."

> "Thou shalt love the Lord thy God with all thy heart, and with all thy soul, and with all thy strength, and with all thy mind; and thy neighbour as thyself."

> "Therefore all things whatsoever ye would that men should do to you, do ye even so to them; for this is the law and the prophets."

> "Pure and undefiled religion before God and the Father is this: To visit the fatherless and widows in their affliction, and to keep himself unspotted by the world."

> "For we know that if our earthly house of this tabernacle were dissolved, we have a building of God, a house not made with hands, eternal in the heavens."

CHAPTER III
The Square

The Holy Bible lies open upon the Altar of Masonry, and upon the Bible lie the Square and Compasses. They are the three Great Lights of the Lodge, at once its Divine warrant and its chief working tools. They are symbols of Revelation, Righteousness, and Redemption, teaching us that by walking in the light of Truth, and obeying the law of Right, the Divine in man wins victory over the earthly. How to live is the one important matter, and he will seek far without finding a wiser way than that shown us by the Great Lights of the Lodge.

The Square and Compasses are the oldest, the simplest, and the most universal symbols of Masonry. All the world over, whether as a sign on a building, or a badge worn by a Brother, even the profane know them to be emblems of our ancient Craft. Some years ago, when a business firm tried to adopt the Square and Compasses as a trade-mark, the Patent Office refused permission, on the ground, as the decision said, that "there can be no doubt that this device, so commonly worn and employed by Masons, has an established mystic significance, universally recognized as existing; whether comprehended by all or not, is not material to this issue." They belong to us, alike by the associations of history and the tongue of common report.

Nearly everywhere in our Ritual, as in the public mind, the Square and Compasses are seen together. If not interlocked, they are seldom far apart, and the one suggests the other. And that is as it should be, because the things they symbolize are interwoven. In the old days when the earth was thought to be flat and square, the Square was an emblem of the Earth, and later, of the earthly element in man. As the sky is an arc or a circle, the implement which describes a Circle became the symbol of the heavenly, or skyey spirit in man. Thus the tools of the builder became the emblems of the thoughts of the thinker; and nothing in Masonry is more impressive than the slow elevation of the Compasses above the Square in the progress of the degrees. The whole meaning and task of life is there, for such as have eyes to see.

Let us separate the Square from the Compasses and study it alone, the better to see its further meaning and use. There is no need to say that the Square we have in mind is not a Cube, which has four equal sides and angles, deemed by the Greeks a figure of perfection. Nor is it the square of the carpenter, one leg of which is longer than the other, with inches marked for measuring. It is a small, plain Square, unmarked and with legs of equal length, a simple try-square used for testing the accuracy of angles, and the precision with which stones are cut. Since the try-square was used to prove that angles were right, it naturally became an emblem of accuracy, integrity, Tightness. As stones are cut to fit into a building, so our acts and thoughts are built together into a structure of Character, badly or firmly, and must be tested by a moral standard of which the simple try- square is a symbol.

So, among Speculative Masons, the tiny try-square has always been a symbol of morality, of the basic Tightness which must be the test of every act and the foundation of character and society.

From the beginning of the Revival in 1717 this was made plain in the teaching of Masonry, by the fact that the Holy Bible was placed upon the Altar, along with the Square and Compasses. In one of the earliest catechisms of the Craft, dated 1725, the question is asked: "How many make a Lodge?" The answer is specific and unmistakable: "God and the square, with five or seven right or perfect Masons." God and the Square, Religion and Morality, must be present in every Lodge as its ruling Lights, or it fails of being a just and truly constituted Lodge. In all lands, in all rites where Masonry is true to itself, the Square is a symbol of righteousness, and is applied in the light of faith in God.

God and the Square - it is necessary to keep the two together in our day, because the tendency of the time is to separate them. The idea in vogue to-day is that morality is enough, and that faith in God - if there be a God - may or may not be important. Some very able men of the Craft insist that we make the teaching of Masonry too religious. Whereas, as all history shows, if faith in God grows dim, morality become, a mere custom, if not a cobweb, to be thrown off lightly. It is not rooted in reality, and so lacks authority and sanction. Such an idea, such a spirit - so wide-spread in our time, and finding so many able and plausible advocates - strikes at the foundations, not only of Masonry, but of all ordered and advancing social life. Once let men come to think that morality is a human invention, and not a part of the order of the world, and the moral law will lose both its meaning and its power. Far wiser was the old book entitled All in All and the Same Forever, by John Davies, and dated 1607, though written by a non-Mason, when it read the reality and nature of God in this manner: "Yet I this form of formless Deity drew by the Square and Compasses of our Creed."

For, inevitably, a society without standards will be a society without stability, and it will one day go down. Not only nations, but whole civilizations have perished in the past, for lack of righteousness. History speaks plainly in this matter, and we dare not disregard it. Hence the importance attached to the Square or Virtue, and the reason why Masons call it the great symbol of their Craft. It is a symbol of that moral law upon which human life must rest if it is to stand. A man may build a house in any way he likes, but if he expects it to stand and be his home, he must adjust his structure to the laws and forces that rule in the material realm. Just so, unless we live in obedience to the moral laws which God has written in the order of things, our lives will fall and end in wreck. When a young man forgets the simple Law of the Square, it does not need a prophet to foresee what the result will be. It is like a problem in geometry.

Such has been the meaning of the Square as far back as we can go. Long before our era we find the Square teaching the same lesson which it teaches us to-day. In one of the old books of China, called The Great Learning, which has been dated in the fifth century before Christ, we read that a man should not do unto others what he would not have them do unto him; and the writer adds, "this is called the principle of acting on the square." There it is, recorded long, long ago. The greatest philosopher has found nothing more profound, and the oldest man in his ripe wisdom has learned nothing more true. Even Jesus only altered it from the negative to the positive form in His Golden Rule. So, everywhere, in our Craft and outside, the Square has taught its simple truth which does not grow old. The Deputy Provincial Grand Master of North and East Yorkshire recovered a very curious relic, in the form of an old brass Square found under the foundation stone of an ancient bridge near Limerick, in 1830. On it was inscribed the date, 1517, and the following words:

"*Strive to live with love and care*
Upon the Level, by the Square."

How simple and beautiful it is, revealing the oldest wisdom man has learned and the very genius of our Craft. In fact and truth, the Square rules the Mason as well as the Lodge in which he labours. As soon as he enters a Lodge, the candidate walks with square steps round the square pavement of a rectangular Lodge. All during the ceremony his attitude keeps him in mind of the same symbol, as if to fashion his life after its form. When he is brought to light, he beholds the Square upon the Altar, and at the same time sees that it is worn by the Master of the Lodge, as the emblem of his office. In the north-east corner he is shown the perfect Ashlar, and told that it is the type of a finished Mason, who must be a Square-Man in thought and conduct, in word and act. With every art of emphasis the Ritual writes this lesson in our hearts, and if we forget this first truth the Lost Word will remain forever lost.

For Masonry is not simply a Ritual; it is a way of living. It offers us a plan, a method, a faith by which we may build our days and years into a character so strong and true that nothing, not even death, can destroy it. Each of us has in his own heart a little try-square called Conscience, by which to test each thought and deed and word, whether it be true or false. By as much as a man honestly applies that test in his own heart, and in his relations with his fellows, by so much will his life be happy, stable, and true. Long ago the question was asked and answered: "Lord, who shall abide in Thy tabernacle? He that walketh uprightly, and worketh righteousness, and speaketh the truth in his heart." It is the first obligation of a Mason to be on the Square, in all his duties and dealings with his fellow men, and if he fails there he cannot win anywhere. Let one of our poets sum it all up:

"It matters not whate'er your lot
Or what your task may be,

One duty there remains for you,
One duty stands for me.
Be you a doctor skilled and wise,
Or do your work for wage,
A laborer upon the street,
An artist on the stage;
One glory still awaits for you,
One honor that is fair,
To have men say as you pass by:
'That fellow's on the square.'

"Ah, here's a phrase that stands for much,
'Tis good old English, too;
It means that men have confidence
In everything you do.
It means that what you have you've earned
And that you've done your best,
And when you go to sleep at night
Untroubled you may rest.
It means that conscience is your guide,
And honor is your care;
There is no greater praise than this:
'That fellow's on the square.'

"And when I die I would not wish
A lengthy epitaph;
I do not want a headstone large,
Carved with fulsome chaff.
Pick out no single deed of mine,
If such a deed there be,
To 'grave upon my monument,
For those who come to see.

Just this one phrase of all I choose,
To show my life was fair:
'Here sleepeth now a fellow who
Was always on the square.' "

CHAPTER IV
The Compasses

In our study of the Square we saw that it is nearly always linked with the Compasses, and these old emblems, joined with the Holy Bible, are the Great Lights of the Craft. If the Lodge is an "oblong square" and built upon the Square (as the earth was thought to be in olden time), over it arches the Sky, which is a circle. Thus Earth and Heaven are brought together in the Lodge - the earth where man goes forth to his labor, and the heaven to which he aspires. In other words, the light of Revelation and the law of Nature are like the two points of the Compasses within which our life is set tinder a canopy of Sun and Stars.

No symbolism can be more simple, more profound, more universal, and it becomes more wonderful the longer one ponders it. Indeed, if Masonry is in any sense a religion, it is Universe Religion, in which ail men can unite. Its principles are as wide as the world, as high as the sky. Nature and Revelation blend in its teaching; its morality is rooted in the order of the world, and its roof is the blue vault above. The Lodge, as we are apt to forget, is always open to the sky, whence come those influences which exalt and ennoble the life of man. Symbolically, at least, it has no rafters but the arching heavens to which, as sparks ascending seek the sun, our life and labor tend. Of the heavenly side of Masonry the Compasses are the symbol, and they are perhaps the most spiritual of our working tools.

As has been said, the Square and Compasses are nearly always together, and that is true as far back as we can go. In the sixth book of the philosophy of Mencius, in China, we find these words: "A Master Mason, in teaching Apprentices, makes use of the compasses and the square. Ye who are engaged in the pursuit of wisdom must also make use of the compass and the square," Note the order of the words: the Compass has first place, and it should have to a Master Mason. In the oldest classic of China, The Book of History, dating back two thousand years before our era, we find the Compasses employed without the Square: "Ye officers of the Government, apply the Compasses." Even in that far off time these symbols had the same meaning they have for us to- day, and they seem to have been interpreted in the same way.

While in the order of the Lodge the Square is first, in point of truth it is not the first in order. The Square rests upon the Compasses before the Compasses rest upon the Square. That is to say, just as a perfect square is a figure that can be drawn only within a circle or about a circle, so the earthly life of man moves and is built within the Circle of Divine life and law and love which surrounds, sustains, and explains it. In the Ritual of the Lodge we see man, hoodwinked by the senses, slowly groping his way out of darkness, seeking the light of morality and reason. But he does so by the aid of inspiration from above, else he would live untroubled by a spark. Some deep need, some dim desire brought him to the door of the Lodge, in quest of a better life and a clearer vision. Vague gleams, impulses, intimations reached him in the night of Nature, and he set forth and finding a friendly hand to help knocked at the door of the House of Light.

As an Apprentice a man is, symbolically, in a crude, natural state, his divine life covered and ruled by his earthly nature. As a Fellowcraft he has made one step toward liberty and light, and the nobler elements in him are struggling to rise above and control his lower, lesser nature. In the sublime Degree of a Master Mason - far more sublime than we yet realize - by human love, by the discipline of tragedy, and still more by Divine help the divine in him has subjugated the earthly, and he stands forth strong, free, and fearless, ready to raise stone upon stone until naught is wanting. If we examine with care the relative positions of the Square and Compasses as he advanced through the Degrees, we learn a parable and a prophecy of what the Compasses mean in the life of a Mason.

Here, too, we learn what the old philosopher of China meant when be urged Officers of the Government to "apply the Compasses," since only men who have mastered themselves can really lead or rule others. Let us now study the Compasses apart from the Square, and try to discover what they have to teach us. There is no more practical lesson in Masonry and it behoves us to learn it and lay it to heart. As the light of the Holy Bible reveals our relation and duty to God, and the Square instructs us in our duties to our Brother and neighbour, so the Compasses teach us the obligation which we owe to ourselves. What that obligation is needs to be made plain: it is the primary, imperative, everyday duty of circumscribing his passions, and keeping his desires within due bounds. As Most Excellent King Solomon said long ago, "better is he that ruleth his spirit than he that taketh a city."

In short, it is the old triad, without which character loses its symmetry, and life may easily end in chaos and confusion. It has been put in many ways, but never better than in the three great words: self-knowledge, self-reverence, self- control; and we cannot lose any one of the three and keep the other two. To know ourselves, our strength, our weakness, our limitations, is the first principle of wisdom, and a security against many a pitfall and blunder. Lacking such knowledge, or disregarding it, a man goes too far, loses control of himself, and by the very fact loses, in some measure, the self-respect which is the corner stone of a character. If he loses respect for himself, he does not long keep his respect for others, and goes down the road to destruction, like a star out of orbit, or a car into the ditch.

The old Greeks put the same truth into a trinity of maxims: "Know thyself; in nothing too much; think as a mortal"; and it made them masters of the art of life and the life of art. Hence their wise Doctrine of the Limit, as a basic idea both of life and of thought, and their worship of the God of Bounds, of which the Compasses are a symbol. It is the wonder of our human life that we belong to the limited and to the unlimited. Hemmed in, hedged about, restricted, we long for a liberty without rule or limit. Yet limitless liberty is anarchy and slavery. As in the great word of Burke, "it is ordained in the eternal constitution of things, that a man of intemperate passions cannot be free; his passions forge their fetters." Liberty rests upon law. The wise man is he who takes full account of both, who knows how, at all points, to qualify the one by the other, as the Compasses, if he uses them aright, will teach him how to do.

Much of our life is ruled for us whether we will or not. The laws of nature throw about us their restraining bands, and there is no place where their writ does not run. The laws of the land make us aware that our liberty is limited by the equal rights and liberties of others. Our neighbour, too, if we fail to act toward him squarely may be trusted to look after his own rights. Custom, habit, and the pressure of public opinion are impalpable restraining forces which we dare not altogether defy. These are so many roads from which our passions and appetites stray at our peril. But there are other regions of life where personality has free play, and they are the places where most of our joy and sorrow lie. It is in the realm of desire, emotion, motive, in the inner life where we are freest and most alone, that we need a wise and faithful use of the Compasses.

How to use the Compasses is one of the finest of all arts, asking for the highest skill of a Master Mason. If he is properly instructed, he will rest one point on the innermost centre of his being, and with the other draw a circle beyond which he will not go, until he is ready and able to go farther.

Against the littleness of his knowledge he will set the depth of his desire to know, against the brevity of his earthly life the reach of his spiritual hope. Within a wise limit he will live and labour and grow, and when he reaches the outer rim of the circle he will draw another, and attain to a full-orbed life, balanced, beautiful, and finely poised No wise man dare forget the maxim, "In nothing too much," for there are situations where a word too much, a step too far, means disaster. If he has a quick tongue, a hot temper, a dark mood, he will apply the Compasses, shut his weakness within the circle of his strength, and control it.

Strangely enough, even a virtue, if unrestrained and left to itself, may actually become a vice. Praise, if pushed too far, becomes flattery. Love often ends in a soft sentimentalism, flabby and foolish. Faith, if carried to the extreme by the will to believe, ends in over-belief and superstition. It is the Compasses that help us to keep our balance, in obedience to the other Greek maxim: "Think as a mortal" — that is, remember the limits of human thought. An old mystic said that God is a circle whose centre is everywhere, and its circumference nowhere. But such an idea is all a blur. Our minds can neither grasp nor hold it. Even in our thought about God we must draw a circle enclosing so much of His nature as we can grasp and realize, enlarging the circle as our experience and thought and vision expand. Many a man loses all truth in his impatient effort to reach final truth. It is the man who fancies that he has found the only truth, the whole truth, and nothing but the truth, and who seeks to impose his dogma upon others, who becomes the bigot, the fanatic, the persecutor.

Here, too, we must apply the Compasses, if we would have our faith fulfil itself in fellowship. Now we know in part - a small part, it may be, but it is real as far as it goes - though it be as one who sees in a glass darkly. The promise is that if we are worthy and well qualified, we shall see God face to face and know ever as we are known. But God is so great, so far beyond my mind and yours, that if we are to know Him at all truly, we must know Him together, in fellowship and fraternity. And so the Poet-Mason was right when he wrote:

"He drew a circle that shut me out,
Heretic, rebel, a thing to flout;
But love and I had the wit to win,
We drew a circle that took him in."

CHAPTER V
The Level and the Plumb

Like the Square and the Compasses, the Level and the Plumb are nearly always united in our Ritual. They really belong together, as much in moral teaching as in practical building. The one is used to lay horizontals, the other to try perpendiculars, and their use suggests their symbolism. By reason of their use, both are special working tools of the Fellowcraft, along with the Square; and they are also worn as jewels by two of the principal officers of the Lodge.

Among the Craft Masons of olden time the actual work of building was done by Fellowcrafts, using materials gathered and rough hewn by Apprentices, all working under the guidance of the Master. In our symbolism, as the Apprentice is youth, so the Fellowcraft is manhood, the time when the actual work of life must be done on the Level, by the Plumb and Square. Next to the Square and Compasses, the Level and Plumb are among the noblest and simplest symbols of the Craft, and their meaning is so plain that it hardly needs to be pointed out. Yet they are so important, in use and meaning, that they might almost be numbered among the Lesser Lights of the Lodge.

I. The Level

The Level, so the newly made Mason is taught, is for the purpose of proving horizontals. An English writer finds a lesson in the structure of the Level, in the fact that we know that a surface is level when the fluid is poised and at rest.

From the use of the Level he bids us seek to attain a peaceful, balanced poise of mind, undisturbed by the passions which upset and sway us one way or the other. It is a counsel of perfection, he admits, but he insists that one of the best services of Masonry is to keep before us high ideals, and, what is more, a constantly receding ideal, otherwise we should tire of it.

Of course, the great meaning of the Level is that it teaches equality, and that is a truth that needs to be carefully understood. There is no little confusion of mind about it. Our Declaration of American Independence tells us that all men are "created equal," but not many have tried to think out what the words really mean. With most of us it is a vague sentiment, a glittering generality born of the fact that all are made of the same dust, are sharers of the common human lot, moved by the same great faith and fears, hopes and loves - walking on the Level of time until Death, by its grim democracy, erases all distinctions and reduces all to the same level.

Anyone who faces the facts knows well enough that all men are not equal, either by nature or by grace. Our humanity resembles the surface of the natural world in its hills and valleys. Men are very unequal in physical power, in mental ability, in moral quality. No two men are equal; no two are alike. One man towers above his fellows, as a mountain above the hills. Some can do what others can never do. Some have five talents, some two, and some but one. A genius can do with effortless ease what it is futile for others to attempt, and a poet may be unequal to a hod-carrier in strength and sagacity. When there is inequality of gift it is idle to talk of equality of opportunity, no matter how fine the phrase may sound. It does not exist.

By no glib theory can humanity be reduced to a dead level. The iron wrinkles of fact are stubborn realities. Manifestly it is better to have it so, because it would make a dull world if all men were equal in a literal sense. As it is, wherein one lacks another excels, and men are drawn together by the fact that they are unequal and unlike. The world has different tasks demanding different powers, brains to devise, seers to see, hands to execute, prophets to lead. We need poets to inspire, scientists to teach, pioneers to blaze the path into new lands. No doubt this was what Goethe meant when he said that it takes all men to make one man, and the work of each is the glory of all.

What, then, is the equality of which the Level is the symbol ? Clearly it is not identity or even similarity of gift and endowment. No, it is something better; it is the equal right of each man to the full use and development of such power as he has, whatever it may be, unhindered by injustice or oppression. As our Declaration of Independence puts it, every man has an equal and inalienable right to "life, liberty and the pursuit of happiness," with due regard for the rights of others in the same quest. Or, as a famous slogan summed it up: "Equal rights for all; special privileges to none!" That is to say, before the law every man has an equal right to equal justice, as before God, in whose presence all men are one in their littleness, each receives equally and impartially the blessing of the Eternal Love, even as the sun shines and the rain falls on all with equal benediction.

Albert Pike, and with him many others, have gone so far as to say that Masonry was the first apostle of equality in the true sense. One thing we do know: Freemasonry presided over the birth of our Republic, and by the skill of its leaders wrote its basic truth, of which the Level is the symbol, into the organic law of this land. The War for Independence, and the fight for constitutional liberty, might have had another issue but for the fact that our leaders were held together by a mystic tie of obligation, vowed to the service of the rights of man. Even Thomas Paine, who was not a Mason, wrote an essay in honour of an Order which stood for government without tyranny and religion without superstition - two principles which belong together, like the Level and the Plumb. Thus, by all that is sacred both in our Country and our Craft, we are pledged to guard, defend, and practice the truth taught by the Level.

But it is in the free and friendly air of a Lodge of Masons, about an altar of obligation and prayer, that the principle of equality finds its most perfect and beautiful expression. There, upon the Level, the symbol of equality, rich and poor, high and low, prince and plain citizen - men of diverse creeds, parties, interests, and occupations - meet in mutual respect and real regard, forgetting all differences of rank and station, and united for the highest good of all. "We meet upon the Level and part upon the Square"; titles, ranks, riches, do not pass the Inner Guard; and the humblest brother is held in sacred regard, equally with the brother who has attained the highest round of the wheel of fortune.

Every man in the Lodge is equally concerned in the building of the Temple, and each has his work to do. Because the task demands different gifts and powers, all are equally necessary to the work, the architect who draws the plans, the Apprentice who carries stones or shapes them with chisel and gavel, the Fellowcraft who polishes and deposits them in the wall, and the officers who marshal the workmen, guide their labor, and pay their wages. Everyone is equal to every other so long as he does good work, true work, square work. None but is necessary to the erection of the edifice; none but receives the honor of the Craft; and all together know the joy of seeing the Temple slowly rising in the midst of their labors. Thus Masonry lifts men to a high level, making each a fellow-worker in a great enterprise, and if it is the best brotherhood it is because it is a brotherhood of the best.

II. The Plumb

The Plumb is a symbol so simple that it needs no exposition. As the Level teaches unity in diversity and equality in difference, so the Plumb is a symbol of rectitude of conduct, integrity of life, and that uprightness of moral character which makes a good and just man. In the art of building accuracy is integrity, and if a wall be not exactly perpendicular, as tested by the Plumb-line, it is weak and may fall, or else endanger the strength and stability of the whole, just so, though we meet upon the Level, we must each build an upright character, by the test of the Plumb, or we weaken the Fraternity we seek to serve and imperil Its strength and standing in the community.

As a workman dare not deviate by the breadth of a hair to the right or to the left if his wall is to be strong and his arch stable, so Masons must walk erect and live upright lives. What is meant by an upright life each of us knows, but it has never been better described than in the 15th Psalm, which may be called the religion of a gentleman and the design upon the Trestleboard of every Mason:

"Lord, who shall abide in Thy tabernacle? Who shall dwell in Thy holy hill? He that walketh uprightly, and worketh righteousness, and speaketh the truth in his heart. He that backbiteth not with his tongue, nor doeth evil to his neighbour, nor taketh up a reproach against his neighbour. In whose eyes a vile person is condemned; but he honoureth them that fear the Lord. He that sweareth to his own hurt, and changeth not. He that putteth not out his money to usury, nor taketh reward against the innocent. He that doeth these things shall never be moved."

What is true of a man is equally true of a nation. The strength of a nation is its integrity, and no nation is stronger than the moral quality of the men who are citizens. Always it comes back at last to the individual, who is a living stone in the wall of society and the state, making it strong or weak. By every act of injustice, by every lack of integrity, we weaken society and imperil the security and sanctity of the common life. By every noble act we make all sacred things more sacred and secure for ourselves and for those who come after us. The prophet Amos has a thrilling passage in which he lets us see how God tested the people which were of old by the Plumb-line; and by the same test we are tried:

"Thus He showed me: and, behold, the Lord stood upon a wall made by plumb-line, with a plumb- line in His hand. And the Lord said unto me, Amos, what seest thou?' And I said, A plumb-line.' Then said the Lord, 'Behold, I will set a plumb- line in the midst of my people of Israel: I will not again pass them by any more."

CHAPTER VI
The Master's Piece

In the olden time it was no easy matter for a man to become a Freemason. He had to win the right by hard work, technical skill, and personal worth. Then, as now, he had to prove himself a freeman of lawful age and legitimate birth, of sound body and good repute, to be eligible at all. Also, he had to bind himself to serve under rigid rules for seven years, his service being at once a test of his character and a training for his work. If he proved incompetent or unworthy, he was sent away.

In all operative Lodges of the Middle Ages, as in the guilds of skilled artisans of the same period, young men entered as Apprentices, vowing absolute obedience, for the Lodge was a school of the seven sciences, as well as of the art of building. At first the Apprentice was little more than a servant, doing the most Menial work, and if he proved himself trustworthy and proficient his wages were increased; but the rules were never relaxed, "except at Christmastime," as the Old Charges tell us, when there was a period of freedom duly celebrated with feast and frolic.

The rules by which an Apprentice pledged himself to live, as we find them recorded in the Old Charges, were very strict. He had first to confess his faith in God, vowing to honour the Church, the State and the Master under whom he served, agreeing not to absent himself from the service of the Order save with the license of the Master. He must be honest and upright, faithful in keeping the secrets of the Craft and the confidence of his fellows. He must not only be chaste, but must not marry or contract himself to any woman during the term of his apprenticeship. He must be obedient to the Master without argument or murmuring, respectful to all

Freemasons, avoiding uncivil speech, free from slander and dispute. He must not frequent any tavern or ale-house, except it be upon an errand of the Master, or with his consent.

Such was the severe rule under which an Apprentice learned the art and secrets of the Craft. After seven years of study and discipline, either in the Lodge or at the Annual Assembly (where awards were usually made), he presented his "Masterpiece," some bit of stone or metal carefully carved, for the inspection of the Master, saving, "Behold my experience!" By which he meant the sum of his experiments. He had spoiled many a bit of stone. He had dulled the edge of many a tool. He had spent laborious nights and days, and the whole was in that tiny bit of work. His masterpiece was carefully examined by the Masters assembled and if it was approved he was made a Master Mason, entitled to take his kit of tools and go out as a workman, a Master and Fellow of his Craft. Not, however, until he had selected a Mark by which his work could be identified, and renewed his Vows to the Order in which he was now a Fellow.

The old order was first Apprentice, then Master, then Fellow - mastership being, in the early time, not a degree conferred, but a reward of skill as a workman and of merit as a man. The reversal of the order today is due, no doubt, to the custom of the German Guilds, where a Fellow Craft was required to serve two additional years as a journeyman before becoming a Master. No such custom was known in England. Indeed, the reverse was true, and it was the Apprentice who prepared his masterpiece, and if it was accepted, he became a Master. Having won his mastership, he was entitled to become a Fellow - that is, a peer and Fellow of the Craft which hitherto he had only served. Hence, all through the Old Charges, the order is "Masters and Fellows," but there are signs to show that a distinction was made according to ability and skill.

For example, in the Matthew Cooke MS. we read that it had been "ordained that they who were passing of cunning should be passing honoured," and those less skilled were commanded to call the more skilled "Masters." Then it is added, "They that were less of wit should not be called servant nor subject, but Fellow, for nobility of their gentle blood." After this manner our ancient Brethren faced the fact of human inequality of ability and initiative. Those who were of greater skill held a higher position and were called Masters, while the masses of the Craft were called Fellows. A further distinction must be made between a "Master" and a "Master of the Work," now represented by the Master of the Lodge. Between a Master and the Master of the Work there was no difference, of course, except an accidental one; they were both Masters and Fellows. Any Master could become a Master of the Work provided he was of sufficient skill and had the fortune to be chosen as such either by the employer or the Lodge, or both.

What rite or ritual, if any, accompanied the making of a Master in the old operative Lodges is still a matter of discussion. In an age devoted to ceremonial it is hard to imagine such an important event without its appropriate ceremony, but the details are obscure. But this is plain enough: all the materials out of which the degrees were later developed existed, if not in drama, at least in legend. Elaborate drama would not be necessary in an operative Lodge. Even to-day, much of what is acted out in an American Lodge, is merely recited in an English Lodge. Students seem pretty well agreed that from a very early time there were two ceremonies, or degrees, although, no doubt, in a much less elaborate form than now practiced. As the Order, after the close of the cathedral-building period, passed into its speculative character, there would naturally be many changes and much that was routine in an operative Lodge became ritual in a speculative Lodge.

This is not the time to discuss the origin and development of the Third Degree, except to say that those who imagine that it was an invention fabricated by Anderson and others at the time of the revival of Masonry, in 1717, are clearly wrong. Such a degree could have been invented by anyone familiar with the ancient Mystery Religions; but it could never have been imposed upon the Craft, unless it harmonized with some previous ceremony, or, at least, with ideas, traditions and legends familiar and common to the members of the Craft. That such ideas and traditions did exist in the Craft we have ample evidence. Long before 1717 we hear hints of "The Master's Part," and those hints increase as the office of Master of the Work lost its practical aspect after the cathedral- building period. What was the Master's Part? Unfortunately we cannot discuss it in print; but nothing is plainer than that we do not have to go outside of Masonry itself to find the materials out of which all three degrees, as they now exist, were developed.

Masonry was not invented; it grew. To-day it unfolds its wise and good and beautiful truth in three noble and impressive degrees, and no man can take them to heart and not be ennobled and enriched by their dignity and beauty. The first lays emphasis upon that fundamental righteousness without which a man is not a man, but a medley of warring passions - that purification of heart which is the basis alike of life and religion. The Second lays stress upon the culture of the mind, the training of its faculties in the quest of knowledge, without which man remains a child. The Third seeks to initiate us, symbolically, into the eternal life, making us victors over death before it arrives. The First is the Degree of Youth, the Second the Degree of Manhood, the Third the consolation and conquest of Old Age, when the evening shadows fall and the Eternal World and its unknown adventure draw near.

What, then, for each of us to-day, is meant by the Master's Piece? Is it simply a quaint custom handed down from our ancient Brethren, in which we learn how an Apprentice was made a Master of his Craft? It is that indeed, but much more. Unless we have eyes to see a double meaning everywhere in Masonry, a moral application and a spiritual suggestion, we see little or nothing. But if we have eyes to see it is always a parable, an allegory, a symbol, and the Master's Piece of olden time becomes an emblem of that upon which every man is working all the time and everywhere, whether he is aware of it or not-his character, his personality, by which he will be tested and tried at last. Character, as the word means, is something carved, something wrought out of the raw stuff and hard material of life. All we do, all we think, goes into the making of it. Every passion, every aspiration has to do with it. If we are selfish, it is ugly. If we are hateful, it is hideous. William James went so far as to say that just as the stubs remain in the check book, to register the transaction when the check is removed, so every mental act, every deed becomes a part of our being and character. Such a fact makes a man ponder and consider what he is making out of his life, and what it will look like at the end.

Like the Masons of old, apprenticed in the school of life, we work for "a penny a day." We never receive a large sum all at once, but the little reward of daily duties. The scholar, the man of science, attains truth, not in a day, but slowly, little by little, fact by fact. In the same way, day by day, act by act, we make our character, by which we shall stand judged before the Master of all Good Work. Often enough men make such a bad botch of it that they have to begin all over again. The greatest truth taught by religion is the forgiveness of God, which erases the past and gives another chance. All of us have spoiled enough material, dulled enough tools and made enough mistakes to teach us that life without charity is cruel and bitter.

Goethe, a great Mason, said that talent may develop in solitude, but character is created in society. It is the fruit of fellowship. Genius may shine aloof and alone, like a star, but goodness is social, and it takes two men and God to make a brother. In the Holy Book which lies open on our altar we read: "No man liveth unto himself; no man dieth unto himself." We are tied together, seeking that truth which none may learn for another, and none may learn alone. If evil men can drag us down, good men can lift us up. No one of us is strong enough not to need the companionship of good men and the consecration of great ideals. Here lies, perhaps, the deepest meaning and value of Masonry; it is a fellowship of men seeking goodness, and to yield ourselves to its influence, to be drawn into its spirit and quest, is to be made better than ourselves.

Amid such influences each of us is making his Master's Piece. God is all the time refining, polishing, with strokes now tender, now terrible. That is the meaning of pain, sorrow, death. It is the chisel of the Master cutting the rough stone. How hard the mallet strikes, but the stone becomes a pillar, an arch, perhaps an altar emblem. "Him that overcometh, I will make a pillar in the temple of my God. "The masterpiece of life, at once the best service to man and the fairest offering to God, is a pure, faithful, heroic, beautiful Character.

> *"Oh! the Cedars of Lebanon grow at our door,*
> *And the quarry is sunk at our gate;*
> *And the ships out of Ophir, with golden ore,*
> *For our summoning mandate wait;*
> *And the word of a Master Mason*

May the house of our soul create!

"While the day hath light let the light be used,
For no man shall the night control!
Or ever the silver cord be loosed, Or broken the golden
bowl, May we build King Solomon's Temple
In the true Masonic Soul!"

CHAPTER VII
The Rite of Destitution

Nothing in Freemasonry is more beautiful in form or more eloquent in meaning than the First Degree. Its simplicity and dignity, its blend of solemnity and surprise, as well as its beauty of moral truth, mark it as a little masterpiece. Nowhere may one hope to find a nobler appeal to the native nobilities of man. What we get out of Freemasonry, as of anything else depends upon our capacity, and our response to its appeal; but it is hard to see how any man can receive the First Degree and pass out of the Lodge room quite the same man as when he entered it.

What memories come back to us when we think of the time when we took our first step in Freemasonry. We had been led, perhaps, by the sly remarks of friends to expect some kind of horseplay, or the riding of a goat; but how different it was in reality. Instead of mere play-acting we discovered, by contrast, a ritual of religious faith and moral law, an allegory of life and a parable of those truths which lie at the foundations of manhood. Surely no man can ever forget that hour when, vaguely or clearly, the profound meaning of Freemasonry began slowly to unfold before his mind.

The whole meaning of initiation, of course, is an analogy of the birth, awakening and growth of the soul; its discovery of the purpose of life and the nature of the world in which it is to be lived. The Lodge is the world as it was thought to be in the olden time, with its square surface and canopy of sky, its dark North and its radiant East; its centre an Altar of obligation and prayer. The initiation, by the same token, is our advent from the darkness of prenatal gloom into the light of moral truth and spiritual faith, out of lonely isolation into a network of fellowships and relationships, out of a merely physical into a human and moral order. The cable tow, by which we may be detained or removed should we be unworthy or unwilling to advance, is like the cord which joins a child to its mother at birth. Nor is it removed until, by the act of assuming the obligations and fellowships of the moral life, a new, unseen tie is spun and woven in the heart, uniting us, henceforth, by an invisible bond, to the service of our race in its moral effort to build a world of fraternal goodwill.

Such is the system of moral philosophy set forth in symbols to which the initiate is introduced, and in this light each emblem, each incident, should be interpreted. Thus Freemasonry gives a man at a time when it is most needed, if he be young, a noble, wise, time-tried scheme of thought and moral principle by which to read the meaning of the world and his duty in it. No man may hope to see it all at once, or once for all, and it is open to question whether any man lives long enough to think it through - for, like all simple things, it is deep and wonderful. In the actuality of the symbolism a man in the first degree of Freemasonry, as in the last, accepts the human situation, enters a new environment, with a new body of motive and experience. In short, he assumes his real vocation in the world and vows to live by the highest standard of values.

Like every other incident of initiation, it is in the light of the larger meanings of Freemasonry that we must interpret the Rite of Destitution. At a certain point in his progress every man is asked for a token of a certain kind, to be laid up in the archives of the Lodge as a memorial of his initiation. If he is "duly and truly prepared" he finds himself unable to grant the request. Then, in one swift and searching moment, he realizes - perhaps for the first time in his life - what it means for a man to be actually destitute. For one impressive instant, in which many emotions mingle, he is made to feel the bewilderment, if not the humiliation, which besets one who is deprived of the physical necessities of life upon which, far more than we have been wont to admit, both the moral and social order depend. Then, by a surprise as sudden as before, and in a manner never to be forgotten, the lesson of the Golden Rule is taught - the duty of man to his fellow in dire need. It is not left to the imagination, since the initiate is actually put into the place of the man who asks his aid, making his duty more real and vivid.

At first sight it may seem to some that the lesson is marred by the limitations and qualifications which follow; but that is only seeming. Freemasons are under all the obligations of humanity, the most primary of which is to succor their fellow men in desperate plight. As Mohammed long ago said, the end of the world has come when man will not help man. But we are under special obligations to our Brethren of the Craft, as much by the promptings of our hearts as by the vows we have taken. Such a principle, so far from being narrow and selfish, has the indorsement of the Apostle Paul in his exhortations to the early Christian community. In the Epistle to the Ephesians we read: "As we have therefore opportunity, let us do good unto all men, especially unto them who are of the household of faith." It is only another way of saying that "charity begins at home," and for Masons the home is the Lodge.

So, then, the destitute to which this Rite refers, and whose distress the initiate is under vows to relieve, as his ability may permit, are a definite and specific class. They are not to be confused with those who are poverty stricken by reason of criminal tendencies or inherent laziness. That is another problem, in the solution of which Masons will have their share and do their part - a very dark problem, too, which asks for both patience and wisdom. No, the needy which this Rite requires that we aid are "all poor, distressed, worthy Masons, their widows and orphans"; that is, those who are destitute through no fault of their own, but as the result of untoward circumstance. They are those who, through accident, disease or disaster, have become unable, however willing and eager, to meet their obligations. Such are deserving of charity in its true Masonic sense, not only in the form of financial relief, but also in the form of companionship, sympathy and love. If we are bidden to be on our guard against impostors, who would use Masonry for their own ends, where there is real need our duty is limited only by our ability to help, without injury to those nearest to us.

A church, if it be worthy of the name, opens its doors to all kinds and conditions of folk, rich and poor alike, the learned and the unlearned. But a Lodge of Masons is different, alike in purpose and function. It is made up of picked men, selected from among many, and united for unique ends. No man ought to be allowed to enter the Order unless he is equal to its demands, financially as well as mentally and morally, able to pay its fees and dues, and to do his part in its work of relief. Yet no set of men, however intelligent and strong, are exempt from the vicissitudes and tragedies of life. Take, for example, Anthony Sayer, the first Grand Master of the Grand Lodge of England. Towards the end of his life he met with such reverses that he became Tyler of Old King's Arms Lodge, No. 28, and it is recorded that he was assisted "out of the box of this Society." Such a misfortune, or something worse, may overtake any one of us, without warning or resource.

Disasters of the most appalling kind befall men every day, leaving them broken and helpless. How often have we seen a noble and able man suddenly smitten down in mid life, stripped not only of his savings but of his power to earn, as the result of some blow no mortal wit could avert. There he lies, shunted out of active life when most needed and most able and willing to serve. Life may any day turn Ruffian and strike one of us such a blow, disaster following fast and following faster, until we are at its mercy. It is to such experiences that the Rite of Destitution has reference, pledging us to aid as individuals and as Lodges; and we have a right to be proud that our Craft does not fail in the doing of good. It is rich in benevolence, and it knows how to hide its labors under the cover of secrecy, using its privacy to shield itself and those whom it aids.

Yet we are very apt, especially in large Lodges, or in the crowded solitude of great cities, to lose the personal touch, and let our charity fall to the level of a cold, distant almsgiving. When this is so charity becomes a mere perfunctory obligation, and a Lodge has been known to vote ten dollars for the relief of others and fifty dollars for its own entertainment!

There is a Russian story in which a poor man asked aid of another as poor as himself: "Brother, I have no money to give you, but let me give you my hand," was the reply. "Yes, give me your hand, for that, also, is a gift more needed than all others," said the first; and the two forlorn men clasped hands in a common need and pathos. There was more real charity in that scene than in many a munificent donation made from a sense of duty or pride.

Indeed, we have so long linked charity with the giving of money that the word has well nigh lost its real meaning. In his sublime hymn in praise of charity, in the thirteenth chapter of First Corinthians, St. Paul does not mention money at all, except to say "and although I bestow all my goods to feed the poor, and have not charity, it profiteth me nothing." Which implies that a man may give all the money he possesses and yet fail of that Divine grace of

Charity. Money has its place and value, but it is not everything, much less the sum of our duty, and there are many things it cannot do. A great editor sent the following greeting at the New Year:

> "Here is hoping that in the New Year there will be nothing the matter with you that money cannot cure. For the rest, the law and the prophets contain no word of better rule for the health of the soul than the adjuration: Hope thou a little, fear not at all, and love as much as you can."

Surely it was a good and wise wish, if we think of it, because the things which money cannot cure are the ills of the spirit, the sickness of the heart, and the dreary, dull pain of waiting for those who return no more. There are hungers which gold cannot satisfy, and blinding bereavements from which it offers no shelter. There are times when a hand laid upon the shoulder, "in a friendly sort of way," is worth more than all the money on earth. Many a young man fails, or makes a bad mistake, for lack of a brotherly hand which might have held him up, or guided him into a wiser way. The Rite of Destitution! Yes, indeed; but a man may have all the money he needs, and yet be destitute of faith, of hope, of courage; and it is our duty to share our faith and courage with him. To fulfill the obligations of this Rite we must give not simply our money, but ourselves, as Lowell taught in "The Vision of Sir Launfal, " writing in the name of a Great Brother who, though he had neither home nor money, did more good to humanity than all of us put together - and who still haunts us like the dream of a Man we want to be.

> *"The Holy Supper is kept indeed,*
> *In what so we share with another's need;*
> *Not that which we give, but what we share,*
> *For the gift without the giver is bare;*

Who bestows himself with his alms feeds three:
Himself, his hungering neighbour, and Me!"

CHAPTER VIII
The Inn of Year's End

Our Ancient Brethren were Pilgrims as well as Builders; and so are we. The idea of life as a journey runs all through the symbolism of Freemasonry, and to forget that truth is to lose half its beauty. Initiation itself is a journey from the West to the East in quest of that which was lost. The reason why a man becomes a Master Mason is that he may travel in foreign countries, work and receive the wages of a Master.

What is symbolism with us was the actual life of Masons in days of old. An Apprentice presented his masterpiece, and if it was approved, he was made a Master and Fellow. He could then take his kit of tools and journey wherever his work called him, a Freemason - free, that is, as distinguished from a Guild Mason, who was not allowed to work beyond the limits of his city. Thus he journeyed from Lodge to Lodge, from land to land, alone, or in company with his fellows, stopping at inns betimes to rest and refresh himself. Sometimes, as Hope describes in his Essay on Architecture, a whole Lodge travelled together, a band of pilgrim builders.

Like our Brethren in the olden time, we too are pilgrims - life a journey, man a traveller - and each of the Seven Ages is neighbour to the rest; and so the poets of all peoples have read the meaning of life, as far back as we can go. It is a long road we journey together, but there are inns along the way, kept by Father Time, in which we may take lodging for the night, and rest and reflect - like the Inn of Year's End, at which we arrive this month, in which there is goodly company, and much talk of the meaning of the journey and the incidents of the road.

Yes, the winding road is a symbol of the life of man true to fact. Once we are aware of ourselves as pilgrims on a journey, then the people and the scenes about us reveal their meaning and charm. If we forget that life is a Pilgrim's Progress, we have no clue at all to an understanding of it. Strangely enough, when we settle down to be citizens of this world, the world itself becomes a riddle and a puzzle. By the same token, the greatest leaders of the race are the men in whom the sense of being pilgrims and sojourners on the earth is the most vivid. It is the strangers in the world, the manifest travellers to a Better Country, who get the most out of life, because they do not try to build houses of granite when they only have time to pitch a tent, or turn in at an inn.

In the friendly air of the Inn of Year's End, where we make merry for to-night, there is much congratulation upon so much of the journey safely done, and much well-wishing for the way that lies ahead. Also, there is no end of complaint at the aches and ills, the upsets and downfalls, of the road. All kinds of faiths and philosophies mingle, and there is no agreement as to the meaning or goal of the journey. Some think life a great adventure, others hold it to be a nuisance. Many agree with the epitaph of the poet Gay in Westminster Abbey:

"Life is a jest, and all things show it:
I thought so once, and now I know it."

But a Mason, if he has learned the secret of his Craft, knows that life is not a jest, but a great gift, "a little holding lent to do a mighty labor." He agrees with a greater and braver poet who said:

"Away with funeral music - set
The pipe to powerful lips -

The cup of life's for him that drinks,
And not for him that sips."

At the end of an old year and the beginning of a new, we can see that it simplifies life to know that we are pilgrims in a pilgrim world. When a man starts on a journey he does not take everything with him, but only such things as he really needs. It is largely a matter of discrimination and transportation. To know what to take and what to leave is one of the finest arts. It asks for insight, judgment, and a sense of values. One reason why the race moves so slowly is that it tries to take too much with it, weighing itself down with useless rubbish which ought to be thrown aside. Much worthless luggage is carted over the hills and valleys of history, hindering the advance of humanity. It is so in our own lives. Men stagger along the road with acres of land on their backs, and houses and bags of money. Others carry old hates, old grudges, old envies and disappointments, which wear down their strength for nothing. At the end of the year it is wise to unpack our bundle and sort out the things we do not need - throwing the useless litter out the window or into the fire.

How much does a man really need for his journey? If the wisdom of the ages is to be believed, the things we actually need are few, but they are very great. "There abideth Faith, Hope, and Love, these three; and the greatest of these is Love." Brotherly Love, Relief, and Truth, to which let us add Courage, which is the root of every virtue and the only security - what more do we need? In a world where the way is often dim, the road rough, and the weather stormy, we have time only to love and do good. Hate is the worst folly. After all, what do we ask of life, here or hereafter, but leave to love, to serve, to commune with our fellows, with ourselves, with the wonderful world in which we live, and from the lap of earth to look up into the face of God ? Neither wealth nor fame can add anything worth while.

The human procession is endlessly interesting, made up of all kinds of folk - quaint, fantastic, heroic, ignoble, joyous, sorrowful, ridiculous and pathetic - some marching, some straggling through the world. There are Greathearts who patrol the road, and angels who walk with us in disguise - angels, we know them to be, because they believe in us when we do not believe in ourselves, and thus make us do our best. And there are skulkers who shirk every danger and wander to no purpose, like the tramp in a western village who, when asked if he was a traveller, replied:-

"Yep, headed south this trip; Memphis maybe, if I don't lay off sooner. I suppose I'm what you call a bum, partner; but I ain't as bad as some of 'em. I've been hitting the road fer quite a spell, nigh forty years; but I hold a feller has a right to live the way he wants to as long as he lets other folks alone. Anyway, I've had a heap of fun. Oh yes, I might have settled down and got married and raised a lot of kids I couldn't a- took care of, same as a lot of fellers. But I didn't. They say kids come from heaven, so I jest thought I'd leave mine stay there. It keeps me a-hustlin' to look after myself, and handin' out a bit now and then to some poor devil down on his luck. Well, so long, partner."

There is the shirk, the loafer, idle and adrift, living without aim or obligation - trying to slip through and get by. But there are spiritual loafers and moral tramps almost as bad, though they do not flip trains or ask for a "hand-out" at the back door. Any man is a loafer who takes more out of life than be puts into it, leaving the world poorer than be found it. He only has lived who, coming to the All-Men's Inn called death, has made it easier for others to see the truth and do the right.

When we know we are journeymen Masons, seeking a Lodge, we can the better interpret the ills that overtake us. One must put up with much on a journey which would be intolerable at home. Our misfortunes, our griefs are but incidents of the road. Our duties, too, are near at hand. The Good Samaritan had never met the man whom he befriended on the road to Jericho. He did not know his name. He may have had difficulty in understanding his language. None the less, he took him to the next inn, and paid for his keep. Finding his duty by the roadside, he did it, and went on his way. Such is the chivalry of the road, and if a man walks faithfully he will come to the house of God.

Since we pass this way but once, we must do all the good we can, in all ways we can, to all the people we can. There come thoughts of those who walked with us in other days, and have vanished. They were noble and true. Their friendship was sweet, and the old road has been lonely since they went away. Toward the end life is like a street of graves, as one by one those who journey with us fall asleep. But if we walk "the Road of the Loving Heart," and make friends with the Great Companion, we shall not lose our way, nor be left alone when we come at last, as come we must, like all Brothers and Fellows before us, to where the old road dips down into the Valley of Shadows.

It is strange; the soul too is a pilgrim, and must pass on. Walking for a brief time in this vesture of clay, it betakes itself on an unknown journey. A door opens, and the pilgrim spirit, set free, makes the great adventure where no path is. But He who made us Brothers and Pilgrims here will lead us there, and the way He knoweth. No blind and aimless way our spirit goeth, but to Him who hath set Eternity in our hearts. Such thoughts visit us, such faiths and hopes cheer us, gathered in the Inn of Year's End, thinking of the meaning of the way.

> *I go mine, thou goest thine;*
> *Many ways we wend,*
> *Many ways and many days,*
> *Ending in one end.*
>
> *Many a wrong and its crowning song,*
> *Many a road and many an Inn;*
> *Far to roam, but only one home*
> *For all the world to win.*

www.ingramcontent.com/pod-product-compliance
Lightning Source LLC
LaVergne TN
LVHW041458070426
835507LV00009B/671